Gandhi

Lauren Diemer

www.openlightbox.com

Step 1
Go to **www.openlightbox.com**

Step 2
Enter this unique code

NTKDIP6C3

Step 3
Explore your interactive eBook!

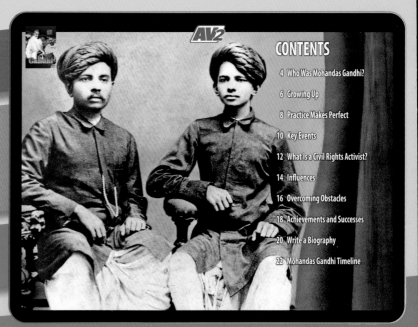

CONTENTS

AV2 is optimized for use on any device

Your interactive eBook comes with...

Contents
Browse a live contents page to easily navigate through resources

Audio
Listen to sections of the book read aloud

Videos
Watch informative video clips

Weblinks
Gain additional information for research

Slideshows
View images and captions

Try This!
Complete activities and hands-on experiments

Key Words
Study vocabulary, and complete a matching word activity

Quizzes
Test your knowledge

Share
Share titles within your Learning Management System (LMS) or Library Circulation System

Citation
Create bibliographical references following the Chicago Manual of Style

This title is part of our AV2 digital subscription

1-Year K–5 Subscription
ISBN 978-1-7911-3320-7

Access hundreds of AV2 titles with our digital subscription.
Sign up for a FREE trial at **www.openlightbox.com/trial**

Gandhi

Contents

Who Was Mohandas Gandhi?

Mohandas Gandhi was a civil rights activist. Among his many achievements, he helped India gain independence from Great Britain. In India, Gandhi is remembered as the "Father of the Nation." He was also known as the Mahatma, or "the great-souled one." Gandhi had many followers and supporters all over the world, especially in India. He worked for fairness and **equality** for the Indian people.

Gandhi believed the best way to bring about change for his people was through **non-violent** means. He would stage hunger strikes as a form of non-violent protest. Gandhi believed a person should not bring harm to any other living being or have many material things. He tried to live by these principles and lead by example.

Over the course of his life, Gandhi became a key figure on the political stage, both in India and internationally. People flocked to his speeches to hear his views on non−violent protest and other issues.

Growing Up

Mohandas Karamchand Gandhi was born on October 2, 1869, in Porbandar, India. Gandhi's father, Karamchand Gandhi, was the *dewan*, or chief minister, of Porbandar. A dewan was a high-ranking politician in India. Gandhi's father did not have much education, but he was a successful politician.

Gandhi's mother, Putlibai, was a very religious woman. She followed the **Hindu** religion. Hindus believe that all life is sacred. This was one reason why Putlibai was a vegetarian. She also believed that everyone should respect one another, regardless of religion.

Gandhi had five siblings. He was closest to his oldest brother, Laxmidas.

Growing up, Gandhi was quite shy. His shyness made it difficult for him to make friends in school. He was also afraid of many things, including the dark. At 13 years old, Gandhi was married to Kasturbai Makanji. It was common for Indian parents to choose a husband or wife for their children.

Gandhi's Birthplace

Porbandar is located in western India, on the coast of the Arabian Sea. It has a population of about 152,000.

India Symbols

TREE
Banyan Tree

BIRD
Indian Peacock

Flower
Lotus

India FACTS

India is the **second most populated** country in the world. More than **1.3 billion people** live there. Only China has more people.

New Delhi was **inaugurated** as **India's capital city** in **1931**.

Mumbai is **India's largest city**. It has a population of about **12.7 million** people.

Practice Makes Perfect

Gandhi went to university in India in 1887. He then decided to go to school in England to become a lawyer. As a lawyer, he could follow in his father's footsteps. In England, Gandhi tried to fit in by adopting the English lifestyle. He wore fancy clothes and took dance lessons, but it did not feel right. He decided to go back to the simple way of life he grew up with in India.

After completing his law degree, Gandhi went home to India. On his return, he had a difficult time. Gandhi learned that his mother had died while he was away. He was also unable to find a job at first. Being shy, he had trouble practicing law. Finally, in 1893, Gandhi accepted a job in South Africa, working on a legal case.

Gandhi was only supposed to practice law in South Africa for one year. Once he learned about the government's law to prevent Indians from voting, he decided to stay longer.

South Africa, like India, was under British rule. Many Indians moved to South Africa to work in mines or on farms. Indians had very few rights in South Africa. They could not vote or own land. When Gandhi wore his traditional turban into a South African courtroom, he was told to remove it. Indians were not allowed to wear hats around white people. He refused and walked out of the courtroom.

Gandhi vowed to get rid of **prejudice** against the Indian people in South Africa. However, he would not use violence to accomplish it. Gandhi's shyness began to disappear. His new sense of purpose gave him strength.

Between 1860 and 1911, as many as 152,000 Indians worked in KwaZulu–Natal, South Africa, on farms, on railways, or in mines.

Key Events

In 1907, the government in the Transvaal region of South Africa passed a law called the Black Act. Under the law, Black and Indian people were not given the same rights as white South Africans. Gandhi refused to obey the law. On November 6, 1913, he led a non-violent protest. More than 2,200 Indian people joined him. Gandhi was arrested for leading the resistance. Before long, 50,000 people were on strike in support of Gandhi's protest. The government knew it could not put that many people in jail. In June 1914, the Black Act was repealed. Gandhi's protest had been successful.

Gandhi returned to India in 1915. Indians in his homeland needed someone to help lead them to independence from Great Britain. Gandhi also wanted equality for India's poor.

Four years after Gandhi's return to India, the British government passed an act in an attempt to stop political unrest. The act permitted Indians to be arrested and held without a trial. It also allowed people to be tried without a jury. In protest of the act, Gandhi led a *hartal*, a nationwide strike.

Gandhi was imprisoned four times while protesting South Africa's laws. His first incarceration, in 1908, was at the Old Fort Prison, on Constitution Hill in Johannesburg.

Thoughts from Gandhi

Mohandas Gandhi strived for equality and freedom in his home country of India. He believed in achieving change through non-violent means.

Gandhi talked about how to achieve happiness.
"Happiness is when what you think, what you say, and what you do are in harmony."

Gandhi believed in helping others.
"The best way to find yourself is to lose yourself in the service of others."

Gandhi defined bravery.
"In the composition of the truly brave there should be no malice, no anger, no distrust, no fear of death or physical hurt."

Gandhi viewed non-violence as a way of overcoming differences.
"Belief in non-violence is based on the assumption that human nature in its essence is one and therefore unfailingly responds to the advances of love…"

Gandhi talked about what makes a person strong.
"Strength does not come from physical capacity. It comes from an indomitable will."

Gandhi believed in the power of action over inaction.
"You may never know what results come of your action, but if you do nothing there will be no result."

What Is a Civil Rights Activist?

Throughout history, groups of people all over the world have been treated unfairly. Civil rights activists, like Gandhi, work to defend the rights of these people. They work to make laws equal for everyone. A civil rights activist attempts to convince local political leaders to change the laws.

Civil rights leaders are often skilled speakers who are able to motivate and inspire people through speeches and arguments. They may organize protests, marches, and **boycotts** to raise awareness about a cause. These protests are meant to put pressure on governments and organizations to change laws.

Civil rights activists sometimes become the focus of anger and frustration. They are often threatened and physically harmed. Some are arrested and spend years in jail. Civil rights activists can also be in danger of assassination.

SATYAGRAHA

Satyagraha was a term Gandhi used to describe his form of protest. It means "insistence on truth" in Hindi. Gandhi introduced satyagraha as a form of non-violent protest.

It involved non-violent methods, such as not cooperating with the **authorities** when a law is unfair. However, satyagraha stressed the importance of being polite and kind. Gandhi believed that, rather than creating change by overwhelming their opponents, people could change their opponents' beliefs through kindness and understanding.

Activists 101

Nelson Mandela
(1918–2013)

Nelson Mandela was an anti–**apartheid** activist in South Africa. He was imprisoned for 27 years for his part in organizing protests against apartheid. Apartheid ended in South Africa in 1991. In 1993, Nelson was awarded the Nobel Peace Prize for his work. He became the country's first black president in 1994.

Martin Luther King, Jr.
(1929–1968)

Martin Luther King, Jr. was a pastor for the Baptist church. He fought to end the **segregation** of African American people in the United States. Martin led several non–violent protests and boycotts in an attempt to change unfair laws. He won the Nobel Peace Prize in 1964, when he was 35. Martin Luther King, Jr. was assassinated on April 4, 1968.

Ayọ Tometi
(1984–)

Ayọ Tometi is an advocate for human rights and social justice. She worked with the Black Alliance for Just Immigration, a group that assists immigrant communities, for many years. In 2013, she co–founded the Black Lives Matter platform to combat racism. Its main focus is to uplift Black communities while reducing the violence these communities often face. Ayọ has received many awards for her efforts and continues to work with communities all over the world.

Malala Yousafzai
(1997–)

Malala Yousafzai is a civil rights activist who fights for the education of women. Malala was born in Mingora, Pakistan, in an area controlled by the Taliban. The Taliban banned girls from attending school. Malala spoke out against the Taliban's restrictions on women's education. In 2012, a Taliban gunman shot Malala. She recovered from the attack, and she continues to fight for women's education. In 2014, Malala received a Nobel Peace Prize.

Influences

Gandhi started a yearlong exchange of letters with Leo Tolstoy after reading Tolstoy's text "A Letter to a Hindu."

Gandhi's mother and her beliefs influenced Gandhi's politics. Putlibai believed that people from all religions should tolerate one another. Gandhi worked very hard for this in his political career. He read books from many religions. He was very influenced by the *Bhagavad Gita*, which contains some of the teachings of Lord Krishna, a Hindu god. Gandhi also read the Koran, an important text about **Islam**, and the Bible, which teaches about **Christianity**.

The writing and ideas of Russian writer Leo Tolstoy were great influences in Gandhi's life. While Tolstoy was Christian, Gandhi grew up believing in Hinduism and **Jainism**. Despite their religious differences, they were good friends and wrote each other regularly.

Gandhi lived in his first ashram, the Sabarmati Ashram, from 1917 to 1930.

In John Ruskin's book *Unto This Last*, Ruskin said wealth was a cause for slavery. He describes manual labor as the only way to live. John Ruskin's book was inspiring for Gandhi, especially when Gandhi was setting up his first **ashram**. Gandhi's ashram followed the principle of using manual labor and literacy as a way of finding purpose in life.

THE GANDHI FAMILY

Mohandas was engaged to Kasturbai at the age of seven. The two were married in 1882. The couple had four sons. Harilal was born in 1887, shortly before Gandhi left for England. Manilal was born in 1892, Ramadas in 1897, and Devadas in 1900. Kasturbai was a great supporter of her husband and his cause. She was imprisoned several times for participating in protests. Kasturbai died in 1944 while under arrest. The couple had been married for 62 years.

Overcoming Obstacles

During the 1919 hartal, some of Gandhi's followers used violence. The British did not like the strike and reacted to the violence. This led to the deaths of more than 350 unarmed Indian people. The Amritsar Massacre caused Gandhi to despair.

In 1918, the spinning wheel became a symbol of freedom when Gandhi urged his followers to make their own cloth instead of buying from English companies.

Beginning in 1920, Gandhi began a boycott of anything from Great Britain. This included all British goods. In 1922, the government sentenced Gandhi to six years in jail for **disobedience** and defying British rule. He served two years in jail, but it did not deter him from his fight.

The British government supplied India with its salt. The government put a very high tax on the salt and would not allow Indians to produce their own. This meant that many Indians could not afford to buy salt. Gandhi tried to change this tax. The government would not **negotiate** with him.

Gandhi started the Salt March with only 78 followers. By the end of the march, thousands had joined his peaceful protest.

On March 12, 1930, Gandhi led a group of people on a march to the sea to challenge the tax. When they reached the sea 24 days later, Gandhi picked up a handful of sea salt. This was against the law. Indians were not allowed to possess salt not purchased from the government. Thousands of Indians began to collect salt from the beach, deliberately breaking the law. More than 60,000 Indians were arrested. Gandhi was put in jail once again.

Achievements and Successes

Eventually, the government accepted the power of Gandhi's non-violent movement. It began negotiating changes to the laws. Gandhi helped reach several settlements with the British government. These changes worked to improve conditions for women and the poor. After a long struggle, India gained independence from Great Britain on August 15, 1947. The British government created two separate countries, dividing the region based on religion. India was primarily Hindu, and Pakistan was created for Muslims. This upset Gandhi, who believed that all religions should accept others' beliefs and live side by side with them as equals. He began a **fast** to remind the people to love, not hate.

On January 30, 1948, Gandhi was assassinated by a **radical** Hindu, Nathuram Godse. Gandhi's death was mourned around the world. In India, approximately one million people followed Gandhi's funeral procession through the streets of Delhi.

In 1931, Gandhi traveled to London, England, for a conference to discuss the future of India with the British government.

During his lifetime, Gandhi was considered a controversial figure. Many people in India loved and respected him. There were also many who did not agree with his beliefs.

Gandhi was nominated for the Nobel Peace Prize five times. However, he never won the award. Over time, Gandhi has become an important figure of tolerance and non-violence. Many other activists have been inspired by Gandhi and his ability to stand up to injustice through peaceful means.

HELPING OTHERS

Gandhi dedicated his life to helping others. As a lawyer, he worked for free to represent the poor. He also worked to heal the sick and wounded. When a plague struck in India, Gandhi helped at the hospital for two hours every day. He also dressed the wounds of people with **leprosy**. During his life, Gandhi set up several ashrams. These spiritual retreats were based on the principles of working and living together as equals.

Write a Biography

A person's life story can be the subject of a book. This kind of book is called a biography. Biographies describe the lives of remarkable people, such as those who have achieved great success or taken important actions to help others. These people may be alive today, or they may have lived many years ago. Reading a biography can help you learn more about a remarkable person.

At school, you might be asked to write a biography. First, decide who you want to write about. You can choose a civil rights activist, such as Mohandas Gandhi, or any other person. Then, find out if your library has any resources about this person. Learn as much as you can about him or her. Write down the key events in this person's life. What was this person's childhood like? What has he or she accomplished? What are his or her goals? What makes this person special or unusual?

A concept web is a useful research tool. Read the questions in the following concept web. Answer the questions in your notebook. Your answers will help you write a biography.

Adulthood

- Where does this individual currently reside?
- Does he or she have a family?

Your Opinion

- What did you learn from your research?
- Would you suggest these books to others?
- Was anything missing from these books?

Childhood

- Where and when was this person born?
- Describe his or her parents, siblings, and friends.
- Did this person grow up in unusual circumstances?

Writing a Biography

Work and Preparation

- What was this person's education?
- What was his or her work experience?
- How does this person work? What is or was the process he or she uses or used?

Main Accomplishments

- What is this person's life's work?
- Has he or she received awards or recognition for accomplishments?
- How have this person's accomplishments served others?

Help and Obstacles

- Did this individual have a positive attitude?
- Did he or she receive help from others?
- Did this person have a mentor?
- Did this person face any hardships? If so, how were the hardships overcome?

Mohandas Gandhi Timeline

Mohandas Gandhi Events		World Events
Mohandas Karamchand Gandhi is born on October 2.	**1869**	The first African American labor union is created in the United States.
Gandhi leads the Transvaal March in South Africa and is arrested.	**1913**	The British House of Commons rejects women's right to vote.
Gandhi returns to India.	**1915**	In New York City, 25,000 women march along Fifth Avenue, demanding the right to vote.
Gandhi leads a march in protest of British control and taxation of salt.	**1930**	In South Africa, white women are given the right to vote.
India wins independence from British rule.	**1947**	Jackie Robinson is the first African American to play in Major League Baseball.
Gandhi is assassinated on January 30.	**1948**	Sri Lanka and Burma, now Myanmar, declare independence from Great Britain.
The United Kingdom releases a commemorative coin that honors Gandhi's life and legacy.	**2021**	Kamala Harris becomes the first woman, the first Black American, and the first South Asian American vice president of the United States.

Key Words

apartheid: a system where white people had more rights than other races

ashram: a building where a spiritual community and its leader live

authorities: the people in control; the people who have the power to control others

boycotts: refusing to use, buy, or participate in something as a way of protesting unfairness

Christianity: the religion based on the teachings of Jesus Christ

disobedience: refusal to obey the laws or rules

equality: the state of being valued the same as others

fast: choosing not to eat

Hindu: related to Hinduism, the dominant religion of India

Islam: a religion that teaches that there is only one God and that Muhammed is God's prophet

Jainism: a religion of India that emphasizes non-violence

leprosy: a disease that affects the skin and nerves and may cause deformity

negotiate: to discuss a problem in order to find a solution

non-violent: peaceful

prejudice: an unfair feeling of dislike for a particular group because of race, religion, gender, etc.

radical: someone or something that departs from tradition

segregation: keeping people of different races separate from one another

Index

Get the best of both worlds.

AV2 bridges the gap between print and digital.

The expandable resources toolbar enables quick access to content including **videos**, **audio**, **activities**, **weblinks**, **slideshows**, **quizzes**, and **key words**.

Animated videos make static images come alive.

Resource icons on each page help readers to further **explore key concepts**.

Published by Lightbox Learning Inc.
276 5th Avenue
Suite 704 #917
New York, NY 10001
Website: www.openlightbox.com

Library of Congress Cataloging-in-Publication Data
Names: Diemer, Lauren, author.
Title: Gandhi / Lauren Diemer.
Description: New York, NY : Lightbox Learning Inc., [2023] | Series: History makers : past and present |
    Includes index. | Audience: Grades 4-6
Identifiers: LCCN 2022001792 (print) | LCCN 2022001793 (ebook) | ISBN 9781791144883 (library binding) |
    ISBN 9781791144890 (paperback) | ISBN 9781791144906
Subjects: LCSH: Gandhi, Mahatma, 1869-1948--Juvenile literature. | Civil rights workers--India--Biography--Juvenile literature. |
    Pacifists--India--Biography--Juvenile literature. | Nonviolence--India--History--20th century--Juvenile literature.
Classification: LCC DS481.G3 D465 2023 (print) | LCC DS481.G3 (ebook) | DDC 954.03/5092 [B]--dc23/eng/20220207
LC record available at https://lccn.loc.gov/2022001792
LC ebook record available at https://lccn.loc.gov/2022001793

Printed in Guangzhou, China
1 2 3 4 5 6 7 8 9 0 26 25 24 23 22

022022
101121

Project Coordinator: Heather Kissock
Designer: Terry Paulhus

Photo Credits
Every reasonable effort has been made to trace ownership and to obtain permission to reprint copyright material. The publisher would be pleased to have any errors or omissions brought to its attention so that they may be corrected in subsequent printings. The publisher acknowledges Alamy, Getty Images, Bridgeman Images, and Newscom as its primary image suppliers for this title.